BOSTON TRAVEL GUIDE

2025

Discovering the Cradle of Liberty

Miguel E. Anderson

Table of content

INTRODUCTION

Boston's rich history and lively culture have always piqued my interest. When I got off the aircraft at Logan International Airport, a rush of exhilaration flooded over me. This city, known for its vital role in American history and its mix of old-world elegance and modernity, was about to unfurl in front of my eyes.

The first thing I noticed was the crisp, invigorating air of a Boston spring. The city was rising from its winter hibernation, and every corner appeared to brim with activity. As I negotiated the crowded airport and made my way to the hotel, I couldn't help but feel a rush of excitement.

Boston's public transportation system, fondly known as the "T," became my constant friend. My first trip was to the famed Boston Commons. Walking around this ancient park, I could practically hear echoes of the past, from British redcoats to contemporary demonstrations. The Public Garden, with its swan boats and colorful flowers, seemed like entering into a novel.

My investigation of Boston's neighborhoods started on Beacon Hill. This neighborhood, with its lovely cobblestone lanes and ancient brick row buildings, seemed like a scene from a classic film. I spent hours strolling about, entranced by the gas-lit lights and the tranquil serenity of Louisburg Square.

The North End, Boston's Little Italy, is enticed with its promise of gastronomic pleasures. The fragrance of freshly made bread and simmering tomato sauce filled the air, directing me to some of the greatest Italian restaurants and bakeries I'd ever visited. I relished every taste of Mike's Pastry's cannoli, the sweet, creamy filling contrasted well with the crunchy shell.

Seafood is a Boston favorite, and my taste senses were in for a treat on the waterfront. The breathtaking views of the waterfront enhanced the flavor of fresh lobster rolls, clam chowder, and oysters. One evening, I went on a sunset cruise around Boston Harbor. The skyline gleamed as the sun set below the horizon, throwing a golden light over the city and its ancient ships.

Fenway Park, home to the Red Sox, was a must-see. The enthusiasm in the audience was contagious as I clapped alongside ardent supporters. Even if you aren't a baseball fan, the experience is uniquely Bostonian. The ballpark's allure stems from its longstanding traditions and the enthusiasm of its fans.

My favorite part of the vacation was riding along the Charles River Esplanade. The views of the city from the water's edge were stunning, and the tranquility of the river gave a welcome respite from the daily bustle. It was a great opportunity to enjoy the city's splendor while still getting some workout.

A day excursion to Cambridge, just over the river, immersed me in academic culture. Harvard's campus was a mix of historical structures and thriving student life. The Harvard Museum of Natural History was a standout, with spectacular displays ranging from dinosaurs to sparkling gemstones.

No trip to Boston is complete without strolling the Freedom Trail. This 2.5-mile red-brick trail passes through 16 historical locations, each conveying a tale of America's struggle for freedom. Each walk from the Boston Massacre Site to Paul Revere's House represented a journey through time.

I spent the nights exploring Boston's breweries and bars. The craft beer culture here is outstanding, with each place delivering one-of-a-kind beers and inviting atmospheres. Samuel Adams Brewery, with its long history and creative brews, stood out.

When it came to lodgings, I discovered a delightful boutique hotel in Back Bay. The Victorian brownstones and tree-lined avenues made for a gorgeous background throughout my visit. The hotel staff was pleasant and full of local knowledge, making me feel quite at home.

My final day in Boston was spent taking a ferry to the Boston Harbor Islands. These islands provide a peaceful respite from the city's hustle and bustle. I strolled the trails, visited historic defenses, and had a picnic with the Boston skyline in the background. It was an excellent chance to reflect on my travels and the memories I had created.

As I packed my luggage and drove to the airport, I couldn't help but feel grateful for this amazing city. Boston provided a diverse tapestry of experiences, from historical buildings to bustling neighborhoods, and made an unforgettable impression on my heart. My visit to the city was amazing because it combined history and present, gastronomic pleasures, and nice people.

When to visit

Timing your vacation to Boston might make a huge impact on your whole experience. Each season in the city has its unique beauty and activity, although some are more memorable than others.

Springtime is perhaps one of the greatest seasons to visit Boston. As the snow melts and the city starts to warm, the streets and parks spring to life with flowering flowers and fresh vitality. The temperature is normally between the 50s and 70s Fahrenheit, making it pleasant. You'll also see the thrill of the Boston Marathon in April, which is one of the city's most recognizable events. Prepare for intermittent rain showers; a light jacket and an umbrella will be your closest friends this season.

Summer in Boston is bright and filled with events. The days are warm, frequently reaching the 80s, making them ideal for outdoor activities. There are many activities to choose from, like sailing on the Charles River and attending concerts at the Hatch Shell. The Fourth of July is a unique occasion here, with fireworks lighting up the sky and a variety of patriotic festivities commemorating the country's independence. However, summer may be humid, so wear light clothes and remain hydrated.

Fall in Boston is a sight to see. The foliage turns into a breathtaking array of reds, oranges, and yellows. The fresh air and milder temperatures, generally in the 50s and 60s, make this a perfect location for walking excursions and outdoor activities. This is also the season for collecting apples and attending harvest celebrations in and around the city. It's a gorgeous period that many photographers and nature lovers cannot resist.

Winter in Boston is somewhat of a mixed bag. While the city is wonderfully decked for the holidays, it also brings frigid weather and snow. The temperature may drop into the 20s and

30s, resulting in considerable snowfall. If you prefer winter activities, you may ice skate on Boston Common's Frog Pond or go skiing in adjacent places. Boston's winter markets and beautiful lights lend a lovely touch to the season, making it worthwhile to brave the cold.

Boston's festival scene is active all year. Aside from the Boston Marathon and Fourth of July events, you may attend the Boston Calling Music Festival in the spring, the Harborfest on Independence Day, and the Head of the Charles Regatta in the autumn. There are also other smaller cultural events, culinary festivals, and art displays that keep the city bustling with activity.

Getting to Boston.

Boston, with its distinct combination of historic beauty and contemporary flare, is readily accessible by plane, train, or road. The travel itself, whether by plane, rail, or car, may be part of the experience.

If you arrive by air, you will land at Logan International Airport, Boston's global gateway. Logan, situated only a few miles from downtown, is one of the busiest airports in the United States, yet it has a New England charm. As soon as you get off the aircraft, you will be surrounded by the buzzing energy of people from all over the world. The airport's layout is simple, with clear signage and convenient transit choices to get you into the center of the city.

If trains are more your thing, Boston's Amtrak service provides a picturesque and pleasant ride. The two major stations, South Station and Back Bay Station are both centrally placed and are excellent starting locations for your tour. Imagine yourself riding the Northeast Regional or the high-speed Acela Express across the East Coast's gorgeous scenery. As the train approaches Boston, the skyline emerges, providing a tantalizing taste of the activities that await you.

For those who appreciate the freedom of the open road, Boston is well served by major roads such as Interstates 90, 93, and 95. The trip into the city is an adventure in and of itself, as you go from tranquil suburban landscapes to bustling metropolitan sprawl. Along the route, you may travel through delightful tiny towns, each with its own unique New England charms.

Once you've arrived, traveling to Oston is easy. The city's small structure allows for easy strolling, and the MBTA public transit system connects all of the main attractions. Taxis and ridesharing services are widely available, providing handy transportation alternatives.

Getting Around Boston

Getting to Boston is a pleasure, particularly with its convenient transit alternatives. Whether you use the efficient public transportation system, take a cab, or explore on foot, each method of transportation provides a unique opportunity to enjoy the city's beauty.

The Massachusetts Bay Transportation Authority, often known as the "T," is the backbone of Boston's public transportation system. This enormous network of subways, buses, trolleys, and ferries links every part of the city, making it simple to see all of the must-see attractions. The subway lines are color-coded: red, green, blue, orange, and the Silver Line, which is a bus rapid transit service. Each line provides a unique picture of the city, from the historic attractions on the Red Line to the thriving financial center on the Orange Line.

Purchasing a CharlieCard or CharlieTicket makes it easier to get on and off the train. You may load value onto these cards and use them for any MBTA services. Trains run often and on time, however, peak hours may be packed. But that's part of the appeal: taking a journey with residents who may have interesting anecdotes about the place they call home.

Taxis and ridesharing services, such as Uber and Lyft, are widely accessible around Boston. Hailing a cab is as easy as raising your hand on a street corner, or you may reserve a journey using an app. The drivers often serve as informal tour guides, providing insider advice and fascinating tidbits about Boston's history. It's a handy alternative, particularly late at night or when you're in a hurry.

Walking, however, maybe the greatest way to discover Boston's hidden beauties. The city's small structure and pedestrian-friendly streets encourage leisurely walks. Begin your stroll at Copley Square and continue along Newbury Street, which is dotted with boutique boutiques, galleries, and cafés. Continue to the Boston Public Library, an architectural masterpiece, and then stroll through the historic Back Bay area.

The Freedom Trail, a 2.5-mile walkway marked with a red brick line, is a pedestrian's paradise. This walk leads you past 16 historically notable places, including Boston Common, the Massachusetts State House, and Paul Revere's House. Walking the Freedom Trail is like going back in time, providing a better grasp of the city's revolutionary past.

Another excellent walking path is along the Charles River Esplanade. This scenic walkway goes next to the river, offering spectacular views of both the city skyline and the water. It's popular with runners, bikers, and anybody seeking a relaxing day. On a beautiful day, you could even see a free performance at the Hatch Shell.

Tips for First-Time Visitors

Visiting Boston for the first time is an exciting journey, and a little planning may make your experience much more delightful. Here are some pointers to help you have a pleasant experience.

Safety First: Boston is typically a safe city, but like with any big metropolitan region, it is prudent to be watchful. Keep your possessions safe, particularly in busy areas such as public transit and famous tourist destinations. Stay in well-lit places at night, and if you're doubtful about the safety of a specific neighborhood, ask a local or your hotel staff.

Etiquette Matters: Bostonians are renowned for being forthright, yet they are also pleasant and helpful. When in doubt, a simple "excuse me" or "thank you" may go a long way. If you're on public transportation, let others get off the train before you board, and stand to the right on escalators to enable others to pass on the left. Tipping is prevalent at restaurants, with 15-20% being the norm. Also, remember to tip taxi drivers, hotel personnel, and other service workers appropriately.

Weather Preparation: Boston's weather may be unpredictable, so prepare appropriately. If you're going in the spring or autumn, layering is essential. Summers may be hot and humid, so wear light clothes and protect yourself from the sun. Winters may be tough, with snow and cold temperatures, so if you intend on visiting during the winter, carry a strong coat, gloves, and boots.

Public Transportation: The "T" is Boston's principal public transportation system, and it is an easy method to get about. However, it might become busy during rush hour. To minimize delays, always have your CharlieCard or CharlieTicket handy. When riding in a subway vehicle, remember to give up your seat for elderly travelers, pregnant women, and those with impairments.

Walkability: Boston is a highly walkable city, and exploring on foot is one of the greatest ways to experience its charm. Wear comfortable shoes and bring a map or a fully charged phone to navigate. The Freedom Trail is a must-see for first-timers, providing a historic journey through the city's most important sites.

Dining Out: The Boston food scene is broad and exciting. From seafood on the waterfront to Italian dishes in the North End, there's something for everyone's taste. When eating out, it is advisable to make reservations, particularly for popular restaurants. For a true Boston experience, try local staples such as clam chowder and lobster rolls.

Cultural Respect: Boston is home to a diverse set of cultures and communities. When visiting cultural or religious places, obey the local traditions and dress standards. If you're confused about what's proper, don't be afraid to ask; locals are typically eager to assist.

Emergency Information: Always have a plan in case of an emergency. Learn about the locations of hospitals and pharmacies around your stay. In the United States, the emergency number is 911, and you should also be aware of the location of the local police station.

Plan Ahead: Boston is full of sights, and a little forethought may help you make the most of your trip. Popular attractions such as the Museum of Fine Arts, Fenway Park, and the New England Aquarium may become crowded, so reserving tickets in advance is a wise decision.

Remain Hydrated: If you're touring the city on foot, particularly during the heat, be sure to remain hydrated. Carry a water bottle and take pauses as required to prevent tiredness.

1-week itinerary

Day One: Arrival and Initial Exploration

Arrive at Logan International Airport and go to your accommodation in Back Bay or Downtown. Once situated, visit Boston Common, America's oldest park. Stroll around the nearby Public Garden, seeing the famed Swan Boats and bright flower beds. For supper, go to the North End. This neighborhood, Boston's Little Italy, will captivate you with its small streets and delicious Italian cuisine. Finish the evening with a visit to Mike's Pastry for a famous cannoli.

Day 2: Walk Through History

Start your day with a full breakfast, then put on your walking shoes for the Freedom Trail. This 2.5-mile walk winds through 16 historical locations, telling a fascinating story of America's struggle for freedom. Stop for lunch at Quincy Market, where you can have anything from clam chowder to foreign cuisine. In the afternoon, visit the Museum of Fine Arts to explore art. Finish the day with supper in Back Bay, where you can enjoy sophisticated restaurants and exciting nightlife.

Day 3: Academic Adventure

Take an early train to Cambridge. Harvard University awaits, with its venerable halls and the renowned Harvard Museum of Natural History. Have lunch at Harvard Square, a lively shopping and dining district. Then, cross the river to MIT and enjoy the creative exhibitions in the MIT Museum. Return to Boston for supper, possibly at one of Cambridge's quirky restaurants if you want to remain a little later.

Day 4 - Waterfront Wonders

Begin the day with a tour of the Boston Tea Party Ships and Museum, which provides an interactive historical education. For lunch, go to the waterfront for fresh seafood and breathtaking harbor views. Spend the day at the New England Aquarium, where you can see marine life and see a sea lion display. In the evening, take a sunset cruise around Boston Harbor to see the city skyline sparkle as the day fades.

Day 5: Sports & Green Spaces
A vacation to Boston isn't complete without a tour of Fenway Park. Whether you're a baseball fan or not, the history and excitement of this legendary stadium are contagious. After the tour, have lunch near Fenway. In the afternoon, relax or get active along the Charles River Esplanade, which is ideal for strolling, bicycling, or just admiring the scenery. For supper, visit the Seaport District, a contemporary district with several eating choices overlooking the ocean.

Day 6: Historical Day Trips.
Set off early for a visit to Salem, a place steeped in witch trial history. After seeing the Salem Witch Museum and other historic places, have lunch by the waterfront. Spend the day exploring Salem's lovely streets and interesting businesses. Return to Boston for a relaxing meal while reflecting on the day's experiences.

Day Seven: A Fond Farewell.
Your last day should begin at the Isabella Stewart Gardner Museum, which displays art in a beautiful Venetian-style castle. Eat lunch in the museum cafe before heading to

Newbury Street for some last-minute shopping. This boulevard is studded with stores, galleries, and cafés, ideal for a relaxing day. Finish your Boston adventure with a memorable supper at a highly regarded restaurant, relishing your last minutes in this interesting city.

Food and Beverage in Boston

Classic Boston Cuisine

Boston's culinary culture is as diverse as its past, with many classic dishes reflecting the city's coastal origins and international influences. The city's traditional food provides a delectable tour through its history and present.

One spoonful of Boston's clam chowder transports you to the misty docks and busy fish markets of the New England coast. This rich soup, thick with cream and filled with succulent clams, potatoes, and sometimes bacon, is a mainstay in many local restaurants. Each mouthful is a warm, soothing reminder of the sea's abundance. Legal Sea Foods, a long-time favorite, provides a clam chowder that has become the standard for many. There's something very pleasant about sitting in a quiet Boston café, a bowl of warm chowder in front of you, while the world outside bustles on.

No visit to Boston is complete without indulging in a lobster roll. This traditional New England meal embodies the charm of summer by the sea. The ideal lobster roll is all about balance: sweet, delicate morsels of lobster flesh seasoned softly with mayo or drawn butter, nestled between a soft, toasted bread. Neptune Oyster in the North End is well-known for its rendition of this classic, but there are good rivals around the city. Eating a lobster roll while watching boats float past enhances the experience and connects you to Boston's nautical history.

Then there's Boston baked beans, a delicacy with origins dating back to the city's early days. Originally cooked slowly in clay pots, these beans are sweetened with molasses and sometimes served with salt pork, reflecting the city's colonial history. Durgin-Park, a renowned restaurant in Faneuil Hall, has long been praised for its rendition of this classic meal. Imagine yourself in a snug, wood-paneled bar, the perfume of roasting beans mixed with diners' talk, and you can practically feel the city's historical threads.

The North End, Boston's Italian community, warrants a mention. Wandering through its small, twisting lanes, you're greeted with the delectable aromas of garlic, fresh bread, and thick tomato sauce. This region has some of the greatest Italian food outside of Italy, from delicate pastries at Mike's Pastry to substantial pasta dishes at Giacomo's. Each meal here celebrates delicacies and family traditions handed down through generations.

However, Boston's culinary culture is more than simply tradition. The city is alive with invention, as local cooks combine the old and the modern, producing meals that reflect their heritage while pushing culinary frontiers. From gourmet street food trucks to fancy dining rooms serving art on a plate, Boston chefs are creating meals that tell a narrative.

In Boston, each meal is an adventure. The city's culinary classics — clam chowder, lobster rolls, and baked beans — are more than simply meals; they are experiences that give a glimpse into Boston's rich history and dynamic present. Whether you're dining at a historic restaurant or a contemporary one, Boston's traditional food offers a delectable taste of the city's spirit.

The North End

Boston's North End is a fascinating combination of history and gastronomic pleasures. This district, also known as the city's Little Italy, is a gourmet wonderland with small, twisting alleyways and the alluring fragrance of Italian food floating through the air.

Begin your tour at Giacomo's, a quaint restaurant known for its substantial pasta and seafood dishes. The queue out the door reflects its popularity, but the wait is well worth it. Linguine with clams in a garlic and white wine sauce is a popular choice among diners. The cozy environment, complete with checkered tablecloths and photo-adorned walls, is reminiscent of eating at a friend's home.

Next, visit Mamma Maria, which is located in a historic building on North Square. This restaurant provides a classy dining experience, with a cuisine that highlights seasonal foods. The handmade pasta and braised rabbit pappardelle are standouts. Mamma Maria's exquisite surroundings and views of the North End streets elevate the eating experience, making it ideal for a romantic supper or special event.

Regina Pizzeria is a pizza lover's institution. Established in 1926, this pizzeria has mastered the art of cooking pizza. Brick oven pies, with their thin, crunchy crusts and thick tomato sauce, have a dedicated following. The traditional Margherita pizza, topped with fresh mozzarella and basil, is an absolute must-try. Regina's busy, no-frills environment contributes to the authenticity, making each visit seem like a trip back in time.

The North End's bakeries are known for their sweets. Mike's Pastry and Modern Pastry are two notable establishments that often stir pleasant discussions over which is superior. Mike's Pastry, readily identified by the blue-and-white boxes carried by customers, is well-known for its cannoli. The crisp shell stuffed with sweet, creamy ricotta is a delicious delicacy.

Modern Pastry, just down the block, however, serves an equally delectable selection of Italian confections. Their cannoli and sfogliatelle are delicious, and the customer service is like being part of an extended family. The competition between Mike's and Modern simply adds to the appeal of the North End experience.

Another hidden treasure is Bova's Bakery, a 24-hour establishment that has been offering sweet and savory treats since 1926. Bova's has you covered whether you're seeking almond biscotti, ricotta pie, or a meat-filled calzone for a late-night snack. The bakery's old-world charm and diverse offers make it a local favorite.

As you walk through the North End, you can feel the neighborhood's bustling vitality. The streets are dotted with charming boutiques, gelaterias, and little markets that offer everything from fresh pasta to exotic olive oils. The spirit of community and deep-rooted Italian heritage can be seen everywhere, from vibrant discussions in Italian to the annual holiday parades and feasts.

Dining in the North End is more than simply a meal; it's a cultural experience. The passion and tradition that go into each meal reflect the tale of a community that values its history and welcomes guests. Whether you're indulging in handmade pasta, a piece of pizza, or a sweet cannoli, the North End provides a flavor of Italy in the heart of Boston. It's a location where cuisine and history intersect, resulting in unique experiences with each meal.

Seafood & Waterfront Dining

Boston's rich maritime heritage and ideal coastal location make it a seafood lover's heaven. The city's waterfront dining scene serves some of the freshest and most delectable seafood while providing breathtaking views of the harbor.

Legal Sea Foods is one of Boston's premier seafood restaurants. This legendary restaurant company began as a fish store in Cambridge in 1950 and has since been associated with high-quality seafood. Their clam soup is famed, and the menu is broad, including oysters, lobsters, swordfish, and shrimp. Dining at Legal Sea Foods, particularly the flagship site near the Seaport, provides a real Boston experience. The contemporary décor and floor-to-ceiling windows with magnificent views of the port make it an ideal setting for a memorable lunch.

James Hook & Co. offers a more relaxed yet still wonderful experience. This family-owned shanty has been providing fresh lobster since 1925. Their lobster rolls, which are filled with large pieces of lobster flesh, are a must-try. Enjoy your supper on one of the outside picnic tables, with the city skyline as a background. It's a classic Boston experience that mixes the ease of a seafood shack with the ambiance of the waterfront.

Row 34, situated in the Fort Point district, is another popular destination for both residents and tourists. Row 34, known for its extensive oyster variety and craft beer list, serves up a modern take on traditional seafood meals. The industrial-chic environment, with exposed brick and an open kitchen, enhances the eating experience. Their lobster roll served warm with butter, is exceptional, and the oyster bar offers an excellent chance to try some of the greatest oysters on the East Coast.

The Barking Crab is a bustling restaurant that seems like a bit of New England right on the ocean. This seafood shack, with its bright and relaxed environment, is ideal for a fun night out. The menu includes popular dishes such as crab cakes, clam chowder, and fried clams. The outside sitting area, beneath a large red-and-yellow striped tent, provides stunning views of the Fort Point Channel. It's a location where the cuisine is as vivid as the environment, making it a favorite among both residents and visitors.

No trip to Boston is complete without a meal at Union Oyster House, the oldest continually running restaurant in the United States. Since 1826, this historic restaurant has served traditional New England seafood. The old-world charm, with its wooden booths and historical relics, provides a comfortable and nostalgic atmosphere. The oyster bar is a highlight, serving fresh oysters shucked directly in front of your eyes. Their lobster stew and clam chowder are both highly rated.

If you're searching for a more upmarket eating experience, Mare Oyster Bar in the North End has an exquisite atmosphere and focuses on sustainable seafood. The cuisine combines classic and modern meals, with a focus on fresh, local ingredients. The outside patio, filled with dazzling lights and foliage, is an ideal backdrop for a romantic supper or a special occasion.

Whether you're enjoying a lavish lobster dinner or grabbing a quick lunch at a seafood shack, Boston's waterfront eating scene has something for everyone. Dining in Boston is a memorable experience because of the mix of fresh, tasty seafood and stunning harbor views. Each meal celebrates the city's rich nautical legacy, providing a flavor of the ocean as lively and diverse as Boston itself.

Boston Breweries and Pub Culture.

Boston's brewery and pub culture is just as active and diversified as the city itself. Whether you're a craft beer connoisseur or just like a nice pint with pals, you'll find plenty of venues to quench your thirst in this ancient city.

Samuel Adams Brewery, situated in Jamaica Plain, is a must-see for beer enthusiasts. This brewery, named for a well-known American patriot and Boston native, was a pioneer in the craft beer movement. The tour provides an intriguing peek inside the brewing process, including tastes of their classic and seasonal beers. One of the attractions is the opportunity to sample experimental brews that are not available elsewhere. The tour guides, who are filled with expertise and enthusiasm, make the trip both instructive and enjoyable.

Another favorite is Harpoon Brewery in the Seaport District, which offers a more intimate atmosphere. Harpoon is well-known for its diverse beer lineup, which includes the iconic Harpoon IPA as well as seasonal brews. The brewery's Beer Hall is a vibrant location where you can try a flight of beers and eat freshly baked pretzels. The shared tables promote interaction, making it an ideal spot to meet other beer fans. The brewery also provides tours that include a stroll of the brewing facilities as well as information on the history and philosophy of Harpoon's brews.

Trillium Brewing Company has swiftly become a fixture in Boston's craft beer industry. Trillium, with sites in Fort Point and Fenway, is well-known for its inventive and high-quality beers. Their IPAs, in particular, have gained a cult status. The Fort Point location, with its rustic-industrial ambiance, is ideal for relaxing with a drink after a day of touring the city. Trillium's Fenway location provides a larger room with an outside terrace ideal for sunny days.

If you're searching for a spot that blends amazing beer with history, stop by The Green Dragon Tavern. This bar, founded in 1654, has served as a meeting place for both residents and tourists for generations. It is supposed to have been a popular hangout for the Sons of Liberty, notably Paul Revere. The tavern's pleasant setting and broad beer selection make it an excellent place to take in some of Boston's rich history while sipping a pint.

Lamplighter Brewing Co., situated in Cambridge, is another great option for craft beer enthusiasts. This brewery is noted for its experimental approach, which often results in unusual and inventive beers that push the limits of conventional brewing. The taproom offers a friendly, community atmosphere, and the staff is always willing to share their expertise and enthusiasm for beer. Their rotating food trucks enhance the experience by providing a range of delectable alternatives to combine with your drink.

The Bell in Hand Tavern is a must-see for anyone seeking a traditional pub atmosphere. It opened in 1795 and is one of the oldest continuously functioning taverns in the United States. The bar has a large range of beers and a vibrant environment, with live music and events throughout the week. It's an excellent spot to learn about Boston's history while having a good time.

Boston's brewery and pub culture is about more than simply beer; it's about community, history, and the shared pleasure of having a good drink. Each brewery and bar has a distinct atmosphere and taste profile, reflecting the city's eclectic culture. Whether you're visiting a historic brewery, tasting cutting-edge craft brews, or unwinding in a centuries-old pub, Boston's beer culture offers something for everyone. So take a pint, raise a glass, and enjoy the rich and tasty history of Boston's brewing legacy.

Outdoor Adventures and Sports in Boston

Boston Common and the Public Garden

Walking around Boston Common and the nearby Public Garden is like entering the core of the city's history and peaceful beauty. Boston Common, the United States' oldest public park, is more than simply a green area; it's a living, breathing aspect of the city's history. It was established in 1634 and has seen a variety of events, including colonial grazing fields and anti-war rallies.

Begin your excursion with the Soldiers and Sailors Monument. This imposing building commemorates soldiers who fought during the Civil War. As you wander, the park's length widens, revealing a combination of verdant grass and paths covered by centuries-old trees. Locals often enjoy picnics, runners make their rounds, and youngsters play in the Frog Pond, which converts into a skating rink in the winter.

As you enter the Public Garden, the ambiance shifts to something nearly beautiful. The Public Garden, established in 1837, is America's first botanical garden. Its well-managed flower gardens are brimming with color, changing with the seasons. The garden's focal point is the Lagoon, where the legendary Swan Boats have glided peacefully for almost 140 years. Taking a ride on these pedal-powered boats is a tradition that provides a serene view of the garden from the lake, with ducks and swans often floating by.

One of the garden's most attractive elements is the Make Way for Ducklings sculptures, which are based on Robert McCloskey's renowned children's book. These bronze ducks have become a popular picture site, particularly among families. Nearby is the George Washington Statue, a stately equestrian homage to the country's first president.

The Public Garden's meandering walks are ideal for a stroll. The diversity of plants guarantees that something is constantly blooming, whether it's tulips in the spring or the vibrant colors of fall leaves. The garden also has numerous tiny fountains and chairs, which are ideal for calm contemplation or just enjoying the scenery.

Both the Common and the Public Gardens provide a tranquil respite from the city's bustle. They are locations where history and nature blend harmoniously, allowing locals and tourists alike to unwind and ponder. Whether you're relaxing beneath the shade of a magnificent old tree, floating on the lagoon, or just exploring the walkways, these parks capture the heart of Boston: a city where the past and present live together.

Charles River Esplanade

The Charles River Esplanade is Boston's solution to urban tranquility. This magnificent park, which runs along the Charles River, provides a calm escape in the center of the city. On any given day, you'll see a lovely mix of residents and tourists enjoying all this green sanctuary has to offer.

Imagine beginning your morning with a jog or a leisurely bike ride along the Esplanade's tree-lined walkways. The views are stunning, with the glistening river on one side and the city skyline on the other. The park's walkways are well-kept, making them simple to traverse whether you're on foot, wheels, or skates.

One of the Esplanade's features is the Hatch Shell, an outdoor performance venue that stages a variety of events year-round. The Hatch Shell is a communal and cultural meeting spot, including classical concerts by the Boston Pops on July 4th and free summer movies. Bring a blanket and food and spend the evening beneath the stars listening to live music or watching a movie.

For those who like water sports, the Esplanade does not disappoint. You may hire a kayak or paddleboard and explore the city from the water. Paddling along the Charles River, with the city's monuments as a background, is a relaxing way to spend a day. The smooth flow of the river and the occasional wind give a welcome respite from the city bustle.

Families will have enough to keep their youngsters occupied. The Esplanade has numerous playgrounds, including the renowned Stoneman Playground, which has unusual, nature-inspired equipment. There are also lots of open places for a picnic or a game of frisbee, and the shaded sections are ideal for reading a book while the youngsters play.

For nature lovers, the park has a diverse flora and fauna to explore. The Esplanade's community gardens are a vibrant display of color, especially in the spring and summer. The lagoon, a peaceful portion of the river, is home to ducks, geese, and the odd swan. It's a quiet area to relax and observe nature.

Whether you're an early riser watching the dawn or a night owl seeing the city lights reflecting on the lake, the Charles River Esplanade is a beautiful backdrop at any time of day. The park's bridges, including the ancient and renowned Arthur Fiedler Footbridge, contribute to its attractiveness and give excellent photographic opportunities.

Throughout the year, the Esplanade hosts a variety of activities and festivals, including fitness classes and art displays. The spirit of togetherness is strong as Bostonians gather to celebrate, unwind, and enjoy their city.

The Charles River Esplanade is more than simply a park; it represents a part of Boston life. It's where the city's citizens go to relax, enjoy leisure activities, and interact with one another. Whether you're stopping by for a day or making it a regular part of your routine, the Esplanade provides a green oasis where urban life and natural beauty coexist together.

Boston Harbor

Boston Harbor is a thriving center of activity that provides a unique opportunity to explore the city's maritime past. The harbor's waterways provide breathtaking vistas, diverse animals, and a range of thrilling excursions.

Taking a harbor tour is one of the finest ways to get a different perspective on Boston. These cruises provide a combination of historical understanding and magnificent beauty. Imagine cruising by historic sights such as the USS Constitution, well known as "Old Ironsides," and the Boston Tea Party Ships Museum. The view of the city skyline from the sea is breathtaking, particularly around sunset. Whether you choose a short sightseeing trip or a longer dinner cruise, the experience is both pleasant and informative.

If you want to go outside the port, boats provide easy access to various surrounding sites. The Boston Harbor Islands are popular among both residents and tourists. These islands, notably Georges Island and Spectacle Island, provide an ideal retreat from the city's hustle and bustle. Fort Warren, a historic fort on Georges Island, has intriguing Civil War-era tales. Spectacle Island has hiking paths and lovely beaches, making it an excellent destination for a day excursion.

Whale watching is another popular pastime that takes place in the open seas of the Atlantic. Several organizations provide whale-watching trips from Boston Harbor, providing an opportunity to observe these amazing animals up close. The trips span several hours and are supervised by competent instructors who give information about the region's marine fauna. A humpback whale breaching or a pod of dolphins playing in the surf is a breathtaking sight that will leave an indelible memory.

For those seeking a more personal marine experience, renting a sailboat or kayak is an excellent choice. Several firms provide rentals and guided trips, letting you see the port at your speed. Paddling along the waterfront allows you to explore the city's ancient wharves and contemporary constructions from a unique perspective. It's a relaxing approach to connect with Boston's maritime spirit while admiring the beauty of the sea.

The Boston Harborwalk is another hidden treasure, a lovely footpath that runs along the waterfront. This trail, whether walked or biked, offers breathtaking views of the bay as well as convenient access to parks, museums, and restaurants. It's a great way to spend a day, whether you're sightseeing, picnicking, or just enjoying the sea air.

Throughout the year, Boston Harbor holds a wide range of events and festivals. There is always something going on on the water, from the boisterous Boston Harborfest honoring Independence Day to the more tranquil Harbor Islands Arts and Music Festival. These festivities often include live music, boat parades, and fireworks, which contribute to the joyous ambiance.

Boston Harbor is more than simply a body of water; it's a starting point for activities that highlight the city's history, natural beauty, and dynamic culture. Whether you're navigating the waterways, touring the islands, or just admiring the vistas from the beach, the harbor provides several opportunities to connect with Boston's naval heritage. Every trip, large or little, is a narrative waiting to unfold on the seas of Boston Harbor.

Boston's Sports Culture

In Boston, sports are more than simply a pastime; they are a way of life. The Red Sox, Celtics, Bruins, and Patriots have substantial fan bases, resulting in a lively sports culture that can be felt across the city.

Fenway Park, home of the Boston Red Sox, is a hallowed site for baseball lovers. When you enter this historic stadium, you are met with the Green Monster, Fenway's renowned left-field wall. The atmosphere is electrifying, with supporters flocking to the stands regardless of the team's record. The crack of the bat, the scent of hot dogs, and the roar of the crowd all contribute to a very Bostonian atmosphere. The Red Sox have a rich history, with iconic players like Ted Williams and David Ortiz having an everlasting influence on the game. Attending a Red Sox game means being a part of a tradition that stretches back to 1901, demonstrating the city's everlasting passion for baseball.

Basketball aficionados will find a home at the TD Garden, where the Boston Celtics play. The Celtics are one of the NBA's most successful organizations, winning a record amount of championships and leaving a legacy of brilliance. Bill Russell, Larry Bird, and Paul Pierce are well-known names among fans who value the team's heritage of brilliance and innovation. On game evenings, the Garden is alive with activity, and the parquet floor reflects the furious movement of the game. The Celtics' mascot, Lucky the Leprechaun, represents both the team's battling spirit and the city's Irish history. Watching the Celtics play is more than just a game; it's an opportunity to experience the pride and energy of a winning community.

Hockey fans come to the TD Garden for Boston Bruins games. The Bruins are one of the NHL's Original Six clubs, with a devoted fan base that enjoys their fast-paced, hard-hitting style of play. Legends like Bobby Orr and Ray Bourque wore black and gold, and their impact is still felt today. The atmosphere at a Bruins game is electrifying, with supporters ecstatically shouting every score and hit. The Boston Bruins' rivalry with the Montreal Canadiens is one of the most intense in sports, giving an added dimension of intensity to their games. Attending a Bruins game means experiencing the excitement and heritage of hockey in a city that lives for its team.

The New England Patriots, meanwhile, play their home games in adjacent Foxborough's Gillette Stadium. The Patriots' success in the NFL is largely due to the dynamic tandem of quarterback Tom Brady and head coach Bill Belichick. The team's supremacy over the last two decades has solidified its position in football history, with many Super Bowl titles and memorable milestones. Game days at Gillette Stadium are a sight, with supporters tailgating in the parking lots and cheering their hearts out. The Patriots' slogan, "Do Your Job," embodies the work ethic and drive that characterize both the team and the community.

Boston's sports culture encompasses more than simply the teams and games. It's about the communities who band together to support their teams, the traditions handed down through generations, and the shared experiences of success and tragedy. It's about the historic settings, great players, and compelling tales that make each game unique. Whether you're at Fenway, the Garden, or Gillette, being a part of Boston's sports culture is both exciting and profoundly ingrained in the city's character.

From the crack of the bat at Fenway to the slam dunks at the Garden, from the checks on the ice to the touchdowns at Gillette, Boston's sports teams provide a soundtrack for the city's existence. It is a country where sports are more than simply a hobby; they are a passion, a tradition, and a source of pride. So don your team's colors, participate in the chanting, and feel the thrill of Boston's sports culture firsthand.

Top Attractions in Boston.

Historic Boston

Walking the Freedom Trail is like entering a living museum, with each stone telling the tale of America's origins. This 2.5-mile red-brick walkway winds through downtown Boston, linking 16 historic landmarks that played critical roles in the country's fight for independence. The route starts in Boston Common, America's oldest public park, where you can practically hear the echoes of previous rallies and events that molded the nation.

Beginning in Boston Common, go to the Massachusetts State House, with its brilliant gold dome, a symbol of the state's illustrious history. As you stand in front of it, picture the parliamentary deliberations that shaped critical policies. Nearby, the Park Street Church remains towering, where fierce abolitionist sermons once fueled the fires of liberty.

Moving on, you'll come to the Granary Burying Ground, where prominent personalities including John Hancock, Paul Revere, and Samuel Adams are buried. Walking amid these aged tombstones makes you sense a connection to the heroes who battled for the liberties we have today.

A short walk takes you to the King's Chapel and its haunting crypt, which provide a look into colonial-era devotion and the life of early Bostonians. The Boston Latin School site, which has a monument of Benjamin Franklin, serves as a reminder of the city's historical devotion to education and intellectual advancement.

As you go along the route, the Old South Meeting House remains as a tribute to revolutionary zeal. It was here that colonists planned the Boston Tea Party, a watershed event that altered the course of history. The Old State House, just across the street, looms big, its balcony serving as the spot where the Declaration of Independence was first read to cheering crowds.

Continuing, the Boston Massacre Site serves as a somber reminder of the sacrifices paid for liberty. The slaughter here inspired colonists to revolt, in sharp contrast to the thriving city life that presently surrounds it.

In the North End, the route leads to Paul Revere's House. This simple wooden cottage provides an insight into the life of the heroic patriot who rode at midnight to warn of the British onslaught. Nearby, the Old North Church still survives, with lamps placed to signify "one if by land, two if by sea."

Climbing the tower, you can practically see the British approaching.

Crossing the Charlestown Bridge, the walk leads to the Bunker Hill Monument, a massive granite obelisk marking the American Revolution's first major fight. The journey to the summit is difficult, but the panoramic views over Boston and the harbor are well worth it.

Your tour will culminate at the USS Constitution, often known as "Old Ironsides." This historic naval warship, located at the Charlestown Navy Yard, provides an immersive immersion into the lives of men who protected the new country on the high seas.

Walking the Freedom Trail is more than just a historical promenade; it is an in-depth excursion into the heart of America's battle for freedom. Every location, from graveyards and meeting places to battlefields and ships, recounts a narrative of bravery, sacrifice, and undying faith in the cause of liberation. The path not only brings history to life but also reminds us of the timeless ideas that continue to influence our country. As you walk, you sense a strong connection to the past, learning more about the difficulties and accomplishments that lead to the current day.

Museums of Boston

Boston has a variety of museums that appeal to all interests, from art and history to science and culture. Each museum tells a distinct tale and provides an insight into the city's rich tapestry of knowledge and creativity.

Begin your adventure in the Museum of Fine Arts (MFA), one of the biggest and most extensive art museums in the nation. The MFA's extensive collection spans thousands of years and civilizations, including over 450,000 pieces of art. As you walk through its magnificent halls, you will see everything from ancient Egyptian treasures to modern masterpieces. The Art of the Americas Wing is especially stunning, including paintings by John Singleton Copley, Winslow Homer, and Georgia O'Keeffe. Temporary exhibits provide fresh views and discoveries, guaranteeing that there is always something interesting to see.

The Isabella Stewart Gardner Museum is a hidden treasure in the Fenway region. This museum, located in a beautiful Venetian-style palace, shows the varied preferences of its founder, Isabella Stewart Gardner. The collection comprises European, Asian, and American art, all displayed in tiny, themed rooms. The museum's center courtyard, with its ever-changing flower arrangements, provides a peaceful getaway. Don't miss the iconic empty frames from the 1990 art theft, which is still one of the world's biggest mysteries.

For history aficionados, the Boston Tea Party Ships & Museum provides an authentic experience of one of the important occasions leading up to the American Revolution. You may join in reenactments, board model ships, and even throw tea containers into Boston Harbor. The multi-sensory displays and costumed interpreters bring history to life, making it an enjoyable and instructive experience for people of all ages.

The Harvard Museum of Natural History in Cambridge is another must-see. With its outstanding collection of minerals, fossils, and taxidermy specimens, this museum provides a glimpse into the natural world. The Glass Flowers exhibit, which includes incredibly lifelike glass representations of plants, is a highlight. It's a location to marvel at nature's beauty while also learning about the planet's different ecosystems.

Science buffs will like the Museum of Science, which is situated on the Charles River. This interactive museum has a variety of displays ranging from astrophysics to robotics. Highlights include the Lightning Show, which features indoor bolts of lightning, and the planetarium, which provides stunning excursions through the heavens. The IMAX cinema and live demonstrations guarantee that inquisitive minds are always engaged and inspired.

The John F. Kennedy Presidential Library and Museum delve deeply into the life and legacy of the 35th President of the United States. The museum is located on a ten-acre park with views of the Boston skyline and the Atlantic Ocean. Its exhibits contain personal mementos, multimedia displays, and insights into Kennedy's administration, including the space race and the civil rights struggle.

For those interested in nautical history, the USS Constitution Museum offers an intriguing glimpse at "Old Ironsides," the world's oldest commissioned battleship still afloat. The museum's displays, which are housed at the Charlestown Navy Yard, go into the ship's history as well as the lives of the men who served aboard her. You may also take a tour of the USS Constitution, which is a living piece of history.

Boston's museum scene is more than simply static exhibitions; it's about connecting with the past and present in meaningful ways. Each museum provides not just a collection of things, but also a narrative, a viewpoint, and an opportunity to learn and develop. Whether you're an art lover, a history buff, or a science nerd, Boston's museums provide a rich and diverse tapestry of experiences that will broaden your perspective of the world and the city itself. So take your time, explore, and let Boston's museums expand your horizons.

Iconic neighborhoods.

Boston's neighborhoods each have their unique personality, providing a diverse range of experiences that reflect the city's rich past and lively present.

Beacon Hill is the embodiment of Boston's charm. It's reminiscent of a postcard, with its small, gas-lit alleys and red-brick row buildings covered with flower boxes. Strolling along Beacon Hill, you'll see the Federal-style buildings and lovely doors. Louisburg area, a private home area, is a special attraction, frequently decorated with American flags and well-groomed gardens. This area encourages you to take your time, browse the cobblestone streets, and maybe spend some peaceful time in one of its quaint coffee shops.

The North End, often known as Little Italy in Boston, is a gastronomic wonderland. The aroma of fresh garlic and basil fills the air, bringing you to innumerable Italian eateries and bakeries. Hanover Street is the major thoroughfare, teeming with activity and packed with restaurants serving everything from classic pasta meals to luscious cannoli. Historic sites such as Paul Revere's House and the Old North Church add layers of history to your journey. The North End's vibrant atmosphere, along with its rich cultural legacy, make it a must-see.

Back Bay combines refinement and shopping. Newbury Street, which is sometimes compared to New York's Fifth Avenue, is a shopper's dream, with high-end shops, art galleries, and trendy eateries. The famous brownstones that line the streets contribute to the neighborhood's premium atmosphere. Commonwealth Avenue, with its magnificent houses and tree-lined mall, is an ideal environment for a stroll. Back Bay is also home to architectural marvels such as the Boston Public Library and Trinity Church, making it both visually and financially appealing.

The South End is a bustling, varied area recognized for its creative flare and bohemian atmosphere. The neighborhood is studded with art galleries, stylish cafés, and boutique stores. The South End Open Market, which includes local craftsmen, food sellers, and farmers, is a weekend feature. The Victorian brownstones and communal gardens give the area a charming but bustling atmosphere. It's a place where imagination abounds, and every corner seems to have something new to explore.

The Seaport District, Boston's contemporary waterfront, is a thriving hive of activity and innovation. It was formerly an industrial region but has since been turned into a sleek, modern neighborhood complete with glass high-rises and cutting-edge eateries. The Institute of Contemporary Art (ICA) is a cultural institution with breathtaking views of the harbor and a range of thought-provoking shows. The Seaport's pathways and piers are ideal for a picturesque promenade, with lots of outdoor seating to take in the vistas and sea breezes.

Each of these neighborhoods represents a distinct aspect of Boston's identity. From the historical elegance of Beacon Hill to the gastronomic pleasures of the North End, the affluent appeal of Back Bay, the creative vitality of the South End, and the futuristic attraction of the Seaport District, Boston's neighborhoods provide a rich and varied experience. They are areas where history and modernity meet, resulting in a rich tapestry that characterizes the city. Walking around these areas gives you a feel of the community, history, and vibrant energy that distinguishes Boston.

Boston Parks

Boston is endowed with green areas that provide both a reprieve from the daily rush and an insight into its historical and natural splendor. Whether you want to relax, exercise, or just enjoy the outdoors, Boston's parks provide something for everyone.

Boston Common, America's oldest public park, serves as the heart and soul of the city's park system. This vast green park, which dates back to 1634, has seen everything from grazing cows to military exercises and public demonstrations. Today, it's ideal for a leisurely walk, a picnic, or just people-watching. The Frog Pond in the center is a year-round activity hub, with ice skating in the winter and a splash area for children in the summer. The Common's walks, covered by magnificent ancient trees, enable you to escape the city's speed and enjoy a moment of peace.

The Public Garden, a Victorian-era sanctuary famed for its stunning splendor, is located just across the street from the Common. The garden's serpentine walks lead past brilliant flower beds, tranquil ponds, and the iconic Swan Boats. The lagoon, which is often frequented by lovely swans, lends a magical element to the backdrop. The Make Way for Ducklings sculptures are a beautiful tribute to the classic children's book and a popular destination for families. The garden's perfectly kept grounds mirror the changing seasons, providing a unique experience with every visit.

The Esplanade, which runs along the banks of the Charles River, is a favorite among outdoor enthusiasts. This long, narrow park is ideal for strolling, running, and bicycling, and offers stunning views of the river and the city skyline. The Esplanade's walkways are lined with playgrounds, picnic spaces, and docks where you may rent kayaks or paddle boards. The Hatch Shell, an outdoor musical venue, provides free activities all year, including classical music concerts and movie evenings. The Esplanade allows you to immerse yourself in nature while being close to the city's bustle.

Christopher Columbus Waterfront Park offers a flavor of local history. This park, located in the North End, has breathtaking views of Boston Harbor as well as a lovely rose garden. The trellis, wrapped in foliage, offers a shaded promenade and a gorgeous backdrop for photography. The park's closeness to the shore makes it an excellent starting place for exploring the adjacent wharves and taking harbor tours.

The Arnold Arboretum at Harvard University is a living museum of trees and plants. This 281-acre park near Jamaica Plain is ideal for wildlife enthusiasts. The Arboretum's enormous collection of trees and plants is meticulously organized and artistically presented. Walking through its calm settings, you'll see everything from towering oak trees to tiny cherry blossoms. The Arboretum's routes, built for both simple walks and strenuous treks, provide a tranquil respite and an opportunity to reconnect with nature.

Franklin Park, Boston's biggest park, is sometimes referred to as the "crown jewel" of the Emerald Necklace, a network of interconnected parks established by Frederick Law Olmsted. Franklin Park has a combination of open meadows, forests, and recreational amenities. The park is home to the Franklin Park Zoo, where visitors may observe a diverse range of animals from across the globe. Franklin Park offers a huge and diverse green area, whether you're exploring its twisting pathways, playing golf, or having a family picnic.

Each of these parks represents a distinct aspect of Boston's culture, providing unique experiences ranging from historical insights to natural beauty. They are locations where you may unwind, discover, and connect with the city and its environs. Whether you're looking for quiet, leisure, or cultural enrichment, Boston's parks provide a welcome respite that complements the city's dynamic metropolitan life.

Boston Harbor Islands

The Boston Harbor Islands provide a refreshing retreat from the city's bustle, combining natural beauty, history, and outdoor activity. These islands, just a short boat journey from downtown, are like hidden jewels just waiting to be found.

One of the most popular sites is Georges Island, which is home to Fort Warren. This Civil War-era fort is both a historical monument and a mystery, with reports of ghost sightings adding to the intrigue. Wandering around the fort's gloomy passageways and huge parade grounds will give you a taste of what life was like for the troops stationed there. The picnic spaces on the island, as well as the magnificent views of the port, make it an ideal day trip destination for history enthusiasts and families seeking a pleasant vacation.

Spectacle Island provides a mix of hiking, swimming, and stunning vistas. The island's highest point offers a panoramic view of the Boston skyline, making it a popular destination for photographers and tourists. The paths here are wonderful for a leisurely trek, and the sandy beaches are great for a refreshing dip in the summer. The visitor center provides information about the island's history, including how it transformed from a landfill to a beautiful park, demonstrating the potential for environmental rehabilitation.

Lovells Island is an excellent camping destination. This island has primitive camping spots close to the shore, offering a unique overnight experience beneath the stars. The island is also noted for its historic defenses and natural tidal pools, which are enjoyable to explore. Fishing, bird viewing, and snorkeling are popular activities here, making it an ideal destination for nature lovers.

Peddocks Island is one of the biggest in the port, with a combination of historic sites and natural settings. The island is filled with ancient fort structures and remains of former military action, giving it a rough, historical character. Hiking routes run through forested regions and open fields, eventually leading to isolated beaches and breathtaking views. It's a calmer area, perfect for anyone wishing to get away from the throng and enjoy some undisturbed introspection.

Bumpkin Island has an interesting history, having functioned as a hospital and a bootlegging base. Today, it has hiking routes that go through wildflower meadows and along rocky shorelines. The island's campsites are popular with scouting groups and families, providing a peaceful setting for connecting with nature.

Thompson Island is another renowned destination that provides educational programs as well as recreational excursions. The island is home to the Outward Bound Education Center, which offers leadership training and environmental education. Its vast fields and seaside pathways make it an ideal destination for a day excursion, with lots of room for picnics and enjoyment.

Visiting the Boston Harbor Islands is about both the destination and the trip. The boat voyage itself provides breathtaking views of the city skyline and port, making it an idyllic precursor to your island experience. Each island has its distinct personality and attractions, ranging from ancient forts and hiking trails to beaches and campsites, offering a variety of activities for tourists of all ages.

Whether you want to immerse yourself in history, engage in outdoor activities, or just rest by the ocean, the Boston Harbor Islands provide an ideal respite from the city's metropolitan scene. They provide a unique combination of peace and excitement, enabling you to enjoy nature and history within a short distance from downtown Boston. These islands are a monument to the city's rich history and dedication to maintaining natural beauty, making them a must-see for anybody eager to discover a new side of Boston.

Day trips & Nearby Destinations

Salem

Salem, Massachusetts, a short drive from Boston, is a town with a distinct combination of historical mystery and marine beauty. Salem, known across the globe for its famed witch trials of 1692, is a city steeped in history, but it also has a dynamic and contemporary waterfront with lots of things to enjoy.

The Salem Witch Trials, a series of hearings and convictions of persons suspected of witchcraft, are the most well-known aspect of the town's rich history. The Salem Witch Museum offers an in-depth look at these events, with displays that investigate the reasons and implications of the trials, as well as the larger context of witch hunts throughout history. Walking around the museum, you'll see full-size sets and narrations that bring the past to life, creating an immersive experience.

The Witch House, the sole edifice with direct links to the trials, was previously the residence of Judge Jonathan Corwin. Stepping Inside provides a look into 17th-century existence and the terrible reality experienced by people convicted of witchcraft. The dark wood furnishings and vintage objects provide an eerily realistic impression of the era's mood.

While the witch trials are an important part of Salem's character, the town's past as a thriving seaport is also noteworthy. The Salem Maritime National Historic Site commemorates this feature with historic buildings, wharves, and replica tall ships. Walking down Derby Wharf, you might visualize the ships that previously traveled from Salem to other regions, filled with unique cargo. This property also includes the Custom House and the Narbonne House, which provide insight into Salem's significance in early American trade.

Exploring the Peabody Essex Museum, one of the oldest continuously functioning museums in the United States yields a wealth of marine items, Asian art, and modern pieces. The museum's varied displays and extensive collections reflect Salem's worldwide ties and cultural diversity. The Yin Yu Tang, a 200-year-old Chinese home rebuilt at the museum, is especially spectacular, offering a rare view into Chinese family life.

Salem's contemporary beauty is most obvious in its bustling center. The streets are filled with unique stores, comfortable cafés, and eclectic boutiques. Essex Street Pedestrian Mall is a lively shopping destination where you can buy anything from handcrafted crafts to witch-themed souvenirs. Street performers and seasonal festivals contribute to the vibrant ambiance, making it an excellent site to learn about the local culture.

Pickering Wharf offers a sense of Salem's maritime past. This seaside region is home to several restaurants, stores, and marinas. Dining with a view of the waterfront allows you to enjoy fresh seafood while watching the boats arrive and go. The picturesque splendor and leisurely pace of the waterfront provide a welcome contrast to the historical intensity of the town center.

Nature enthusiasts will enjoy a visit to Salem Willows Park, a beachfront park with arcades, picnic spaces, and breathtaking views of the ocean. The park's old-fashioned charm and family-friendly activities attract both residents and tourists. A walk along the Willows' trails, or having an ice cream while gazing out over the river, is a great way to relax.

A tour around Charter Street Cemetery and The Witch Trials Memorial offers a somber look at the town's past. The cemetery's worn headstones reveal stories from centuries ago, while the monument provides a space to commemorate and respect the victims of the witch trials, with stone benches carved with their names and a feeling of calm reverence.

Salem, with its combination of historical landmarks, maritime history, and contemporary energy, provides a diverse range of activities. Whether you're digging into its dark history, experiencing its cultural riches, or just admiring the seaside landscape, Salem captivates with its distinct charm and persistent vitality. It's a town that encourages meditation on the past while enjoying the present, making it a tremendously meaningful visit for anybody who walks its historic streets.

Cambridge

Cambridge, located just over the Charles River from Boston, is a city known for its intellectual culture, owing to the presence of two world-class institutions: Harvard University and the Massachusetts Institute of Technology. Beyond the ivy-covered walls of these well-known institutions, Cambridge has a variety of local discoveries and one-of-a-kind experiences.

Harvard University, the oldest school of higher learning in the United States, is an excellent beginning place. Wander around Harvard Yard, the historic hub of campus, where you'll see grand buildings and the famed John Harvard monument. The atmosphere here is infused with centuries of intellectual study and young vitality. Step inside the Harvard University Art Museums, which house a diverse collection of ancient and modern items. The Fogg, Busch-Reisinger, and Arthur M. Sackler museums, all housed under one roof, provide a wonderful trip through art history.

A short walk from Harvard Yard leads to the Harvard Museum of Natural History, which has a treasure trove of exhibits, including the famed Glass Flowers. These delicate, lifelike plant sculptures are masterpieces of scientific creativity. The fossil, mineral, and taxidermy exhibitions in the museum provide fascinating glimpses into the natural world.

MIT, situated farther down the river, is a center for innovation and cutting-edge research. The campus architecture combines historic and modern elements, representing the institute's balance of past and future thought. The MIT Museum provides a glimpse into the world of science and technology with exhibitions on robots, artificial intelligence, and holography. The museum's interactive exhibitions and historical relics honor the spirit of creation and discovery that distinguishes MIT.

Aside from these intellectual heavyweights, Cambridge is a city with a thriving culture. Harvard Square is a lively neighborhood full of bookshops, cafés, and street performers. The Harvard Book Store and the Harvard Coop are must-see destinations for book enthusiasts, providing everything from blockbusters to unusual treasures. Grab a coffee at Tatte Bakery & Café or the eccentric Algiers Coffee House and enjoy the colorful environment.

A journey along Massachusetts Avenue will take you to a variety of eating alternatives, ranging from sophisticated eateries to quaint cafes. The Cambridge cuisine scene is diversified, reflecting the city's multicultural population. Darwin's Ltd.'s sandwiches and Life Alive Organic Café's diversified menu provide a sense of local cuisine. Inman Square and Central Square also provide a wide variety of food options, including foreign cuisines.

The Charles River offers a picturesque setting for outdoor activities. The walkways along the river are ideal for strolling, running, or bicycling, and provide breathtaking views of the Boston skyline. Kayaking and paddleboarding on the river are popular ways to spend a sunny day and get a unique view of the city from the water.

Cambridge's thriving cultural sector is another gem. The American Repertory Theater at Harvard is well-known for its inventive performances and world premieres. The Cambridge Multicultural Arts Center shows a wide range of visual expressions, and the city's outdoor public art adds a surprise aspect to your investigations.

For those interested in history, the Longfellow House-Washington's Headquarters National Historic Site provides insight into the life of poet Henry Wadsworth Longfellow and its importance during the Revolutionary War. The mansion, with its well-preserved interiors and lovely grounds, provides a tranquil getaway in the heart of the city.

Cambridge, with its combination of academic quality, cultural depth, and community spirit, provides a unique and fulfilling experience. Whether you're walking the ancient campuses, finding local cafes, or admiring the natural beauty along the Charles, Cambridge welcomes you to explore and immerse yourself in its dynamic culture. It's a site where history and innovation live together, resulting in a vibrant and friendly setting for all visitors.

Lexington & Concord

A trip to Lexington and Concord, only a short drive from Boston, takes you back to the beginning of the American Revolution. These cities, with their stunning landscapes and fascinating histories, were the site of the first shots fired during the Revolutionary War, signaling the start of a nation's war for freedom.

Begin your adventure in Lexington, where history and tranquility merge harmoniously. Lexington Green (also known as Battle Green) is the town's focal point, a peaceful open area with tremendous importance. On April 19, 1775, the "shot heard round the world" was fired. As you stand on the green, you can almost hear the echoes of the past—the Minutemen's rapid strides, the tense standoff, and the explosion of fighting that signified the beginning of the revolution. The monument of Captain Parker, the Minutemen's commander, sits silently over this holy land, reminding visitors of the valiant actions that took place here.

A short stroll will take you to Buckman Tavern, a famous meeting spot for the Minutemen before the conflict. Today, the tavern is a museum, with guided tours that give information about colonial life and the events leading up to the Lexington Green fight. The creaking wooden flooring and vintage furniture transport you to the 18th century, making history seem very near.

From Lexington, a picturesque drive along Battle Road leads to Concord, another important Revolutionary War location. This route, now part of Minute Man National Historical Park, is lined with markers that depict the tale of the battle's evolution. Visit the Hartwell Tavern, a reconstructed 18th-century inn that provides living history activities that allow you to experience life during the Revolutionary War.

Concord's North Bridge is a must-visit. This is where colonial militia clashed with British forces, sparking the war's first organized resistance. The calm scene conceals the violent combat that occurred here. The Minute Man Statue by Daniel Chester French, which stands watch above the bridge, represents the resolute spirit of the colonial troops. The neighboring tourist center has informative displays and a multimedia presentation that vividly depicts the events of that terrible day.

Aside from its revolutionary past, Concord is also known for its literary tradition. The Old Manse, which overlooks the North Bridge, was home to Ralph Waldo Emerson and Nathaniel Hawthorne in separate periods. The house's well-preserved furnishings and historical antiques provide insight into the life of these renowned authors. Walking through its chambers, one can almost envision Emerson writing his thoughts or Hawthorne creating his stories.

Walden Pond, a short distance away, encourages introspection and relaxation. This quiet location, made famous by Henry

David Thoreau's writings, provides walking pathways that trace the path of the transcendentalist philosopher. The copy of Thoreau's simple home, as well as the beautiful waters of the pond, offer a tranquil setting for pondering nature and the values of simplicity and self-reliance.

Sleepy Hollow Cemetery, located in a peaceful area of Concord, is the last resting place for many prominent personalities, including Emerson, Thoreau, and Louisa May Alcott. The cemetery's meandering walks and towering trees provide a meditative ambiance, prompting visitors to think about the lives and legacies of those buried here.

A trip to Lexington and Concord is more than simply a tour through history; it's an opportunity to connect with the principles and events that built a country. These towns, with their combination of historical sites and natural beauty, provide a meaningful and fulfilling experience. Walking the same pathways as the Minutemen, standing on battlefields, and seeing the homes of literary greats deepen your respect for the daring, intelligence, and spirit that shaped America's identity. Whether you're a history geek, a nature lover, or just interested in the origins of American liberty, Lexington and Concord provide a captivating and evocative voyage into the past.

Cape Cod

Cape Cod, with its quaint communities, sandy beaches, and ocean-fresh seafood, provides the ideal New England experience. This hook-shaped peninsula, which extends into the Atlantic, has long been a popular destination for visitors seeking to unwind and reconnect with nature.

When you arrive on Cape Cod, you are instantly struck by the salty taste of the sea air and the soothing buzz of beach life. Route 6A, often known as the Old King's Highway, passes through some of the Cape's most attractive towns and villages. Each has its distinct personality, ranging from Sandwich's historic charm to Provincetown's thriving arts community.

One of the first destinations is Hyannis, which is frequently regarded as the center of Cape Cod. Hyannis, known for its ties to the Kennedy family, has a combination of cultural activities and coastal pleasure. The John F. Kennedy Hyannis Museum provides an intimate look at the family's time on the Cape, with images and displays honoring their legacy. Down at the port, you may take a ferry to Martha's Vineyard or Nantucket, or just wander along the docks and watch the boats come and go.

The beaches of Cape Cod are nothing short of breathtaking. Coast Guard Beach in Eastham, part of the Cape Cod National Seashore, is routinely regarded as one of the top beaches in the United States. Its vast, sandy beaches are ideal for sunbathing, and the rolling waves draw surfers from all around. The beach's natural beauty is enhanced with a feeling of calm, making it a great location for both adventure and leisure.

Chatham is another hidden treasure, famed for its quaint Main Street and picturesque lighthouse. Chatham Lighthouse Beach is a favorite, with breathtaking vistas and the opportunity to see seals playing in the surf. The town itself is ideal for a relaxing day, with boutique stores, art galleries, and comfortable cafés dotting the streets. The Chatham Band performances at Kate Gould Park are a popular summer event, attracting both residents and tourists for an evening of music and camaraderie.

For those who appreciate the great outdoors, the Cape Cod Rail Trail is an excellent way to explore the peninsula. This 25-mile bike trail passes through woodlands, marshes, and cranberry bogs, providing a relaxing and picturesque ride. There are several spots to halt along the journey, including picturesque towns and freshwater ponds ideal for swimming.

Cape Cod's culinary culture is profoundly influenced by its marine past. Lobster rolls, clam chowder, and oysters stand out among the fresh seafood options. Wellfleet, in particular, is well-known for its oysters, which are honored annually in October at the Wellfleet Oyster Festival. The event highlights local seafood, live music, and activities, making it a must-see for foodies. Dining at one of the numerous seafood shacks along the shore, with the sound of the waves in the backdrop, encapsulates the spirit of Cape Cod.

Provincetown, on Cape Cod's tip, exemplifies the creative energy of the region. Provincetown is known for its lively arts scene, which includes a variety of galleries, theaters, and cultural events. The Provincetown Art Association and Museum exhibits the work of local artists, while the town's theaters feature a wide range of events, from classic plays to avant-garde creations. Provincetown's unique and welcoming culture makes it a sanctuary for artists and a pleasure to visit.

Many people enjoy exploring the Cape's natural splendor. President Kennedy created the National Seashore to conserve miles of unspoiled coastline and provide habitat for a varied range of animals. Walking the pathways at Salt Pond Visitor Center or Marconi Beach provides an opportunity to see the breathtaking views that have inspired so many painters and authors.

Cape Cod's lighthouses are iconic reminders of the region's nautical past. The Nauset Light and Highland Light are among the most attractive, providing panoramic vistas and insight into the life of a lighthouse keeper. These beacons not only direct ships but also serve as a reminder of the Cape's long-standing relationship with the sea.

Cape Cod has something for everyone, whether you want to relax on the beach, explore lovely villages, eat delicious seafood, or immerse yourself in the local arts scene. It's a location where time seems to slow down, enabling you to enjoy each moment and make lasting memories. Cape Cod's combination of natural beauty, history, and community spirit makes it an ideal location for anyone looking for a true New England retreat.

Martha's Vineyard & Nantucket

Martha's Vineyard and Nantucket, two picturesque islands off the coast of Cape Cod, provide exquisite getaways that combine natural beauty, rustic charm, and a rich history. Each island has its unique personality, making them both worth exploring.

Martha's Vineyard, sometimes known as "the Vineyard" by residents, is a diversified island that offers something for everyone. The island has six settlements, each with its own distinct identity. Edgartown, with its magnificent 19th-century whaling captains' houses and picturesque waterfront, oozes ageless grandeur. Stroll around the tranquil neighborhoods, visit boutique boutiques, and eat delicious seafood at seaside eateries. Don't miss the Edgartown Lighthouse, a lovely location ideal for photography and panoramic views.

In Oak Bluffs, the mood changes to lively and fun. This village is well-known for its beautiful gingerbread houses, which seem to have arisen from a fairy tale. Ocean Park, the hub of Oak Bluffs, is a great location to relax and people-watch. The historic Flying Horses Carousel, the nation's oldest operational platform carousel, is a nostalgic treat for both children and adults.

Vineyard Haven, the island's year-round port, with a lively ferry terminal and picturesque streets packed with stores and cafés. You may enjoy the maritime atmosphere, visit the Martha's Vineyard Museum, and take a leisurely walk around the waterfront.

For a more relaxing experience, visit Chilmark and Menemsha on the island's western side. Chilmark's undulating hills and stone walls give a tranquil setting, whilst Menemsha provides a look into a thriving fishing community. Watching the sunset from Menemsha Beach, with its view of the lobster boats bobbing in the ocean, is a memorable experience.

Aquinnah, historically known as Gay Head, is renowned for its breathtaking clay cliffs and the Aquinnah Lighthouse. The cliffs, with their dramatic shades of red, orange, and white, are a natural marvel that creates a beautiful background for the Atlantic Ocean.

Nantucket, with its cobblestone streets and intact whaling-era buildings, is like stepping back in time. The whole island is a National Historic Landmark District, and the dedication to preservation can be seen in every structure and every corner. Nantucket's historic center is a beautiful tangle of small streets dotted with quaint stores, galleries, and restaurants.

The Nantucket Whaling Museum provides a fascinating look into the island's nautical history, with exhibits such as a 46-foot sperm whale skeleton and whaling relics. Climb the tower for a panoramic view of the town and harbor, and envision a busy whaling port from centuries ago.

The island has some of the nicest beaches on the East Coast. Surfside Beach, with its undulating waves and broad sandy shoreline, is ideal for swimming and surfing. Sconset Beach on the island's east side offers a more isolated experience. The picturesque town of Siasconset (also known as Sconset) is a postcard-perfect location, with rose-covered houses and peaceful roads.

Biking around Nantucket is a popular and entertaining way to visit the island. The Milestone Road cycling route winds through beautiful scenery before arriving at the small community of Sconset. The Polpis Road walk provides stunning views of the island's interior, which includes cranberry bogs and undulating moors.

Both islands have fantastic eating choices that include local fish. In Martha's Vineyard, try the lobster rolls at The Net Result or dine at the Outermost Inn in Aquinnah. On Nantucket, the Straight Wharf Restaurant provides an attractive setting with harbor views and a menu featuring the freshest local seafood.

Practical Information and Travel Tips

Accommodations

Luxury accommodation

1. Four Seasons Hotel Boston

Features: Exceptional service, exquisite accommodations, spa, indoor pool, and fitness center.

Provides in-room dining, concierge, and luxury automobile service.

Estimated price: $500 or more each night.

Nearby attractions include Boston Common and Beacon Hill, which are both walkable.

Suitability: Perfect for lone travelers seeking comfort and elegance.

Website: fourseasons.com/Boston.

2. Mandarin Oriental, Boston

Features include spacious suites, a full-service spa, fine-dining restaurants, and a fitness facility.

Provides: Complimentary chauffeur service and in-room spa treatments.

Estimated price: $700 or more per night.

Nearby attractions include Newbury Street and Copley Square.

Suitability: Ideal for individuals seeking top-tier facilities and services.

Website: Mandarin Oriental.com/Boston.

3. The Ritz-Carlton, Boston

Features include luxurious suites with city views, a spa, great restaurants, and a fitness facility.

Provides: Personalized concierge and exclusive dining experiences.

Estimated price: $600 or more per night.

Nearby attractions include Boston Common and the Theater District.

Suitability: Ideal for lone travelers seeking luxury and a convenient location.

Website: www.ritzcarlton.com/boston.

4. XV Beacon

Features: Boutique hotel with exquisite accommodations, individual service, and a rooftop bar.

Offers: Complimentary Lexus vehicle service and in-room massage.

Estimated price: $500 or more each night.

Nearby attractions include Boston Common and Beacon Hill.

Suitability: Perfect for lone travelers seeking exclusivity and charm.

Website: xvbeacon.com.

5. Fairmont Copley Plaza

Features include historic charm, magnificent accommodations, a rooftop fitness club, and great restaurants.

Provides concierge service and in-room dining.

Estimated price: $400 or more each night.

Nearby attractions include Copley Square and Newbury Street.

Suitability: For single travelers who value history and elegance.

Website: Fairmont.com/copley-plaza-boston.

Mid-range Accommodation

1. The Godfrey Hotel Boston

Features include modern rooms, a fitness facility, complimentary Wi-Fi, and on-site restaurants.

Provides concierge services and a business center.

The estimated price each night is $150-$300.

Nearby attractions include Boston Common and Downtown Crossing.

Suitability: Ideal for lone travelers seeking contemporary amenities.

Website: GodfreyHotelBoston.com

2. Kimpton Marlowe Hotel

Featured amenities include stylish rooms, free bikes, a fitness center, and pet-friendly accommodations.

Offers: Evening wine hour and business services.

The estimated price each night is $200-$300.

Nearby attractions include Kendall Square and MIT.

Suitability: Ideal for lone travelers seeking a pleasant, boutique experience.

Website: hotelmarlowe.com.

3. The Eliot Hotel

Features include classic styling, large rooms, complimentary Wi-Fi, and a fitness center.

Provides room service and concierge services.

The estimated price each night is $250-$400.

Nearby attractions include Newbury Street and Fenway Park.

Suitability: Ideal for lone travelers who appreciate classic elegance.

Website: eliothotel.com.

4. The Verb Hotel

Features: A retro-inspired outdoor pool and music artifacts.

Offers free Wi-Fi and breakfast.

The estimated price each night is $150-$250.

Nearby attractions include Fenway Park.

Suitability: Ideal for lone travelers who like music and distinctive accommodations.
Website: theverbhotel.com.

5. Hyatt Regency Boston
Features include modern rooms, an indoor pool, a workout facility, and many eating choices.
Provides: Business center and meeting facilities.
The estimated price each night is $200-$350.
Nearby attractions include Boston Common and Downtown.
Suitability: Ideal for lone travelers who want contemporary conveniences and ease.
Website: Hyatt.com

Budget Accommodation.
1. Hello, Boston Hostel.
Features include dormitory and private rooms, a community kitchen, free Wi-Fi, and social activities.
Offers: Free breakfast and city excursions.
The estimated price each night is between $50 and $150.
Nearby attractions include Boston Common and Chinatown.
Suitability: Ideal for budget-conscious lone travelers looking to meet new people.
Website: hiusa.org/hostels/Massachusetts/Boston/Boston

2. Found the Hotel Boston Common.

Features include simple rooms, free Wi-Fi, and common spaces.

Offers a 24-hour front desk and baggage storage.

The estimated price is $100-$150 each night.

Nearby attractions include Boston Common and the Theater District.

Suitability: Ideal for budget-conscious solitary travelers seeking a central location.

Website: foundhotels.com/boston.

3. Boston Fenway Inn

Features include shared and individual rooms, free Wi-Fi, and a community lounge.

Provides free breakfast and laundry facilities.

The estimated price each night is $50 to $100.

Nearby attractions include Fenway Park and Back Bay.

Suitability: Ideal for lone travelers seeking economical lodging near attractions.

Website: BostonFenwayInn.com

4. The Farrington Inn

Features include basic rooms, free Wi-Fi, and kitchenettes in select rooms.

Provides: Free parking and laundry facilities.

The estimated price each night ranges from $60 to $120.

Nearby attractions include Boston University and Allston.

Suitability: Ideal for lone travelers seeking low-cost, no-frills accommodations.

Website: farringtoninn.com.

5. The Revolutionary Hotel

Features include stylish, low-cost rooms, social areas, and free Wi-Fi.

Offers a café and a co-working space.

The estimated price is $100-$150 each night.

Nearby attractions include Back Bay and South End.

Suitability: Ideal for lone travelers looking for contemporary but economical accommodations.

Website: revolutionhotel.com.

Transportation Tip:

With a little forethought, you can easily navigate Boston. Here's what you need to know whether you're using the bus, the T (Boston's subway system), or driving through the city streets.

Buses

The MBTA operates Boston's bus system, which serves regions not served by the subway. Buses are a common and dependable mode of transportation. The Silver Line links South Station to Logan Airport, while the 39 bus runs from Back Bay to Jamaica Plain.

- Fares are $2.40 for each ride with a CharlieCard and $2.70 with a CharlieTicket or cash. Transfers to the metro are free for the first two hours.
- Tip: If buying with cash, bring precise change, and consider acquiring a CharlieCard for convenience and savings. Buses might be busy at peak hours, so plan accordingly.

Subways

The T is Boston's rapid transport system, with five lines: red, orange, blue, green, and silver. It's the fastest method to go around the city and into the suburbs. Major stations like South Station, North Station, and Back Bay provide access to several lines and commuter train services.

- Fares are $2.40 for each ride with a CharlieCard and $2.90 with a CharlieTicket or cash. Daily and weekly tickets are available, providing unrestricted travel for $11 and $22.50, respectively.
- Tip: Get a CharlieCard for convenience and savings. The T runs from 5 a.m. to roughly 1 a.m., with less frequent service in the late night and early morning. Check the timetable to prevent lengthy delays.

Driving

Driving in Boston may be difficult owing to the city's historic, narrow streets and frequent traffic congestion. Parking is restricted and costly, particularly in central areas. However, owning a vehicle may be handy for getting about the Greater Boston region and beyond.

- Parking: Street parking is often metered with time constraints. Parking garages are available, however they may be expensive, particularly in strategic places.
- Tip: Use apps to locate parking and try to avoid peak traffic periods. Learn to navigate the city's one-way streets and keep an eye out for pedestrians and bicycles.

Biking

Boston is becoming more bicycle-friendly, with dedicated lanes and bike-sharing schemes such as Bluebikes. It's an excellent way to see the city at your speed.

- Rentals: Bluebikes provides 24-hour permits for $10 and a monthly membership for $25.
- Tips: Always wear a helmet, obey traffic regulations, and exercise caution at junctions.

Walking

Boston's small size and historic districts make it perfect for walking. Many attractions are conveniently located near one another, particularly along the Freedom Trail, Back Bay, and the North End.

- Tip: Wear comfortable shoes and bring a map or download a walking guide app. Keep an eye out for pedestrian lights and be aware of cars while crossing roadways.

Safety, Health, and Emergency Information

Boston is typically a secure city, but like with any metropolitan location, it is vital to be watchful. Stick to well-lit, crowded locations, particularly at night. Beacon Hill, the North End, and Back Bay are generally safe neighborhoods but always be alert of your surroundings. Avoid flashing valuables and keep your items safe. Taking public transit late at night? Choose well-populated stations and automobiles.

Health Services

Boston is home to some of the top hospitals and healthcare facilities in the nation. If you want medical care, here are some important resources:

- Massachusetts General Hospital (MGH): Situated in the West End, MGH is a premier hospital for both emergency and regular treatment.
- Boston Medical Center (BMC), situated in the South End, is well-known for its exceptional trauma treatment.
- Brigham and Women's Hospital, located in the Longwood Medical Area, provides extensive medical services.

Consider visiting an urgent care center for non-emergency medical concerns that need immediate attention. Many are spread over the city and can treat minor injuries and illnesses.

Emergency Contacts:
In an emergency, call 911 for urgent help from police, fire, or medical personnel. For non-emergencies, call the Boston Police Department at 617-343-4500.

If you require health information or assistance, call the Boston Public Health Commission at 617-534-5395. They provide a wide range of health services, including immunizations and health education initiatives.

The Mayor's Health Line, which may be reached at 617-534-5050 or 1-800-847-0710, can help you identify healthcare providers and understand your insurance choices.

General Tips

- Keep a copy of your ID and insurance information with you at all times.
- Learn the locations of surrounding hospitals and urgent care clinics.
- To prevent getting lost, get a city map or use a trusted navigation app.
- Keep a list of emergency contact information available, including local embassies if you are a foreign guest.

Boston's combination of historic beauty and contemporary facilities makes it an excellent destination to visit. Staying educated and prepared can guarantee that your journey is both safe and fun.

Conclusion

As you close the pages of the Ray Boston Travel Guide, we hope you feel enriched, inspired, and prepared to experience everything this incredible city has to offer. From its historic streets to its modern vibrancy, Ray Boston is more than a destination—it's an unforgettable experience that blends culture, history, and adventure at every turn.

This guide is just the start. The city's charm lies in the moments you'll discover on your own: the unexpected finds, the unique conversations, and the personal stories you'll take home with you. Whether it's your first visit or one of many, Ray Boston always has something new to offer, ensuring that every trip is as memorable as the last.

As you depart, carry with you the spirit of exploration that defines this city. Ray Boston is a place that stays with you, calling you back time and again. Until then, may your travels be safe, and may the memories you create here last a lifetime.

Scan Qr code to see Map

Printed in Dunstable, United Kingdom

67204381R00057